Jesus Raises the Widow's Son

Luke 7:11–17, 31 for Children

Written by Nicole E. Dreyer
Illustrated by Dave Hill

CONCORDIA PUBLISHING HOUSE · SAINT LOUIS

In Jesus' time it wasn't safe
For a woman to live alone.
Without a husband or a son,
She'd be lost and poor on her own.

So if a widow's son would die,
She would be in great distress;
For without a man to care for her,
She'd be left in quite a mess!

Then in the town of Nain one day,
Where a widow's son had died,
The entire town went to her house
To comfort her as she cried.

And when it was time to bury him
They placed him on a bier—
A special stretcher that was used
To carry the body so dear.

They lifted the bier and began to walk
With a slow and somber gait
To the cemetery on the other side
Of the town; to Nain's main gate.

But as they reached the gate they saw
A crowd of people draw near:
It was Jesus with His twelve apostles
And others who'd followed Him here.

When the Lord saw the mourners with the bier
And the widow walking beside,
His heart was touched by her sorrow and pain,
So He said to her, "Don't cry."

The people heard Jesus speaking to her
As they stopped there on the road;
Then the Lord Himself came closer to them
And touched their heavy load!

"Young man, I say to you, get up!"
The Lord said to the boy.
And that's exactly what he did
As his mother cried with joy!

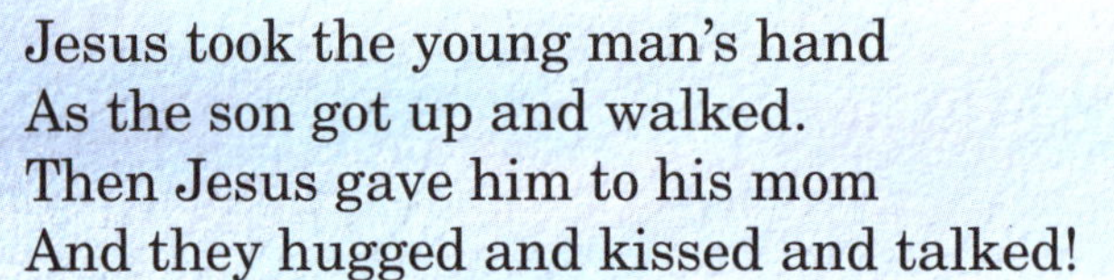

Jesus took the young man's hand
As the son got up and walked.
Then Jesus gave him to his mom
And they hugged and kissed and talked!

The people there who witnessed this
Were shocked and filled with awe!
They celebrated this miracle
And sang their praises to God.

"A prophet has come to us," they said.
"He is surely someone great!"
"God has come to help us all—
Let's spread the word; don't wait!"

So the news of this great miracle
Was spread from town to town.
They heard it throughout Judea
And in the country all around:

That Jesus had raised the widow's son—
Had brought him back to life!
This showed His power over death
And revealed that He was the Christ!

And still today the news is spread:
It's carried around the world.
In every land and every tongue,
God's message is unfurled.

Because Jesus, our Lord, is Christ the King;
Over Satan, Christ won the fight!
Defeating death, forgiving our sins,
And giving us eternal life!

Dear Parent:

As more people heard Jesus preach, more of them came to believe that He was the Messiah. In the Bible story immediately preceding this one, Luke tells us that a centurion knew who Jesus was and asked Him to heal his servant. Jesus "marveled" at this Gentile's strong faith.

In this story, Jesus and His followers came upon a funeral procession. The mother of the dead young man was overcome with grief. Our compassionate Lord was moved by her anguish and reached out to help her. Touching the bier, though, meant that according to Jewish Law, Jesus made Himself ceremonially unclean. This deliberate act would have shocked everyone who saw it.

But the thing Jesus did next shocked them even more. By raising this man from the dead, Jesus proved He was God in the flesh and had authority over death. Imagine how quickly word of this miracle would have spread.

What is interesting about this event is that Jesus did not wait for someone to ask Him to act. He immediately took compassion on the widow and acted for her benefit. Jesus comforted her with His words, and He provided for her.

When you read this book with your child, point out that because He loves us, Jesus always has compassion on us, even when we're not aware that we need it. He comforts us with His words. And by His death on the cross, Jesus provides for our greatest need—forgiveness of our sins.

The Editor